CW01512596

Original title:

Opaline Visions Inside the Faerie Hearth

Author: Aron Pilviste

ISBN HARDBACK: 978-1-80562-763-0

ISBN PAPERBACK: 978-1-80564-284-8

Dreams Wrapped in Dappled Glow

In twilight's tender clasp we find,
Our secrets whispered in the wind.
With starlit paths, our hearts entwined,
Through forest realms, our dreams ascend.

The moonlight dances on the leaves,
A melody of soft embrace.
In magic's weave, the spirit weaves,
A tapestry of time and space.

Beneath the hazel's watchful eye,
We chase the sparks of fleeting thought.
With every sigh and whispered goodbye,
In dappled light, our fortunes sought.

The shadows zoom and flicker bright,
Where wishes bloom and softly glow.
In silence deep, we chase the night,
Dreams wrapped in dappled, golden flow.

We rise with dawn, our hearts anew,
Of every star, a tale unfolds.
With every dream, a world so true,
In dappled light, our hope beholds.

Lanterns of the Whispering Woods

In glades where shadows softly creep,
The lanterns flicker, tales set free.
With every step, the old trees weep,
Their whispered truths, a sage decree.

Through tangled paths, the moonlight streams,
Illuminating joy and fright.
With each embrace, the forest beams,
A symphony of dark and light.

The owls begin their nightly round,
With wisdom perched upon their wings.
In secret glens, we roam unbound,
Lost in the magic that night brings.

The lanterns sway as wishes rise,
A soft glow in a world so wide.
Through whispering woods, beneath the skies,
Our hearts and stories two, allied.

Beneath the stars, our laughter dances,
With every trail, a new delight.
In nature's arms, pure joy enhances,
We find our way through darkened night.

Cascades of Enchanted Radiance

In mountains high where eagles soar,
The cascades sing, their spirits fly.
With every rush, we yearn for more,
The magic weaves through earth and sky.

A prism bright in every spray,
Reflecting dreams anew and bold.
In glistening flow, we chase the day,
With laughter like the waters rolled.

The river paints with colors rare,
A canvas wrought from nature's hand.
Each droplet whispers, soft and fair,
In gleaming tales that roam the land.

In harmony, our spirits twine,
As rivers dance upon the stone.
Through cascades bright, our hearts align,
In shared enchantment, never alone.

We stand where echoes find their grace,
In radiant dreams, we dare to thrive.
Cascades of light, our hearts embrace,
In nature's flow, we come alive.

Hearthstone Hues Beyond the Veil

At evening's hearth, the stories glow,
In whispers held by warm embrace.
With flames that dance in amber flow,
We share our dreams in sacred space.

The shadows sway, the embers gleam,
Each flicker tells of yesteryears.
In every crackle, hope and dream,
A tapestry of loves and fears.

Within the walls, the memories breathe,
As laughter echoes soft and bright.
In every heart, a thread we weave,
Hearthstone hues in gentle light.

Beyond the veil, the spirits roam,
In twilight's dance, they intertwine.
Where once was loss, now feels like home,
With every breath, their voices shine.

In warmth we gather, hand in hand,
To share our tales, both new and old.
In hearthstone hues, we understand,
The bonds of love, the stories told.

Unveiling Dreamscapes by the Fireside

In whispers soft, the tales begin,
Around the fire, where dreams take wing.
Shadows flicker, the night ignites,
A tapestry woven of magical sights.

Forgotten realms come forth to play,
In ember's glow, they dance and sway.
A world of wonder, bright and bold,
As stories of old in warmth unfold.

The clock ticks slow, as wonders blend,
With every crackle, the journeys mend.
Curved and twisted, the paths we trace,
Diving deep into the dreamscape's embrace.

Each heartbeat syncs with the fire's call,
A timeless echo that binds us all.
Through twilight's veil, our visions soar,
In every spark, we seek for more.

So gather 'round, let the magic reign,
For by the fire, we'll break the chain.
With every tale, a heart takes flight,
In the dreamscapes unveiled by the night.

Fantastical Whimsy in Crystalline Hues

In a world adorned with glittering light,
Whimsy dances on the edge of night.
Crystals shimmer with secrets untold,
As stories in laughter and wonder unfold.

Petals of magic in pastel shades,
Whispering hopes as twilight fades.
Waves of color that swirl and glide,
A fantastical canvas, where dreams abide.

Butterflies flit in the gentle breeze,
Drawing the heart towards joyful unease.
Each brush of wind tells tales anew,
In this realm of crystalline hue.

Stars twinkle softly, a celestial quest,
Inviting all souls to come and rest.
In the embrace of enchantment's fold,
A tapestry rich, with stories of old.

So lose yourself in the hues so bright,
Where whimsy dances, a pure delight.
In every corner, the magic sways,
In fantastical realms, let hearts ablaze.

Where Enchantment Meets the Night

In the tranquil hush, the moonlight sings,
A gentle echo of mystical things.
Stars wheeling slowly, secrets in flight,
Where dreams unfurl just out of sight.

The night air whispers, soft and clear,
Calling forth wonders that draw us near.
In shadows deep, enchantments gleam,
A realm of magic, alive with dream.

Every rustle or shimmer holds a tale,
Of brave hearts sailing on the night's pale.
With paths aglow and lanterns bright,
Together we wander, lost in delight.

From starlit corners, visions arise,
With promises woven across the skies.
Hand in hand with celestial might,
We traverse the magic where dreams ignite.

So linger awhile, in this mystic embrace,
Let the enchantments guide us in grace.
For in the night where wonders alight,
We find our place, where dreams take flight.

Threads of Light in Arcane Shadows

In the silence of night, where shadows reside,
Threads of light twine, weaving wide.
With whispers of magic, they softly dance,
Entwining the heart in a cosmic romance.

Mysteries murmur in twilight's embrace,
Shrouded in darkness, they find their place.
A flicker of hope in the deepening gloom,
With every heartbeat, a spark to bloom.

Celestial weavers spin tales in the air,
Guiding the lost through realms of despair.
In their luminous glow, we find our way,
As dreams take shape at the dawning of day.

With gentle resolve, the shadows recede,
And light intertwines with each whispered deed.
In each fragile thread, a story unfolds,
Of love everlasting, and journeys untold.

So follow the threads, let your spirit ignite,
In the depths of the night, where shadows hold tight.
For within every dark, a brilliance shines bright,
As we weave our hopes through the threads of light.

Spheres of Wonder and Iridescence

In twilight's hush, the hues arise,
Like whispers spun from evening skies.
A dance of light on velvet ground,
Where dreams of magic can be found.

Each orb, a secret, softly shared,
A tale of hope, of hearts ensnared.
They twinkle bright with ancient lore,
Inviting souls to seek and explore.

Through crickets' song, a gentle cue,
The world transforms in shades anew.
With every breath, enchantment swells,
In hidden nooks, where wonder dwells.

The moon casts shadows, long and deep,
Where hidden memories softly creep.
Embracing night with tender grace,
While stars above begin to race.

So seek the spheres, embrace the night,
With open hearts, bathe in their light.
For in their glow, you'll find the key,
To worlds untold, to setting free.

Molten Fantasia in the Grotto

Beneath the stone, where echoes dwell,
Awaits a tale we long to tell.
With every drop, the cave ignites,
A molten dream in shadowed nights.

Cascading pools of shimmering gold,
Where whispers of the past unfold.
In twilight's grip, the magic blooms,
Dispelling gloom in hidden rooms.

With crystalline walls that softly gleam,
Each glimmer stirs a wondrous dream.
As creatures dance through misty haze,
Lost in their waltz of ancient days.

The stories held in silver streams,
Are windows wide to whispered dreams.
As fireflies weave their gentle spell,
Through every curve, there's magic to tell.

So venture forth, and you may find,
A molten heart that's intertwined.
In every flicker, every splash,
The grotto sings with vibrant flash.

Threads of Luminescence in the Air

In twilight's veil, the threads entwine,
A tapestry of spark and shine.
They weave through whispers, soft and light,
A symphony of day and night.

With every breath, they spiral clear,
A melody for hearts to hear.
As golden strands of sunlit grace,
Waltz through the world, a warm embrace.

They flutter near, like dreams set free,
In every flutter, possibility.
With every spark, a wish is spun,
From dreams of many, one by one.

Through gentle night and morning's rise,
These strands of light ignite the skies.
For in their glow, the truth we find,
A link that binds both heart and mind.

So follow forth on whispered trails,
Where luminescence never pales.
In threads of light, our hopes remain,
A dance of joy, a sweet refrain.

The Glow that Holds Sylvan Stories

In ancient woods where shadows play,
The glow reveals what hides away.
With every glimmer, tales unfold,
Of creatures brave and hearts so bold.

Amidst the leaves, the lanterns sway,
As whispers paint the night with day.
Each flicker tells a tale of yore,
Of magic found on the forest floor.

The owls take flight with silent grace,
As fireflies brighten the secret place.
With rustling leaves and gentle sighs,
The woods awake beneath the skies.

Among the roots where moonbeams kiss,
Lies hidden realms of endless bliss.
In shadows deep, the stories bind,
A world of wonder for the kind.

So wander forth, where glow persists,
In sylvan tales that twist and twist.
For in the dusk, we chance to find,
The hearts of stories intertwined.

A Faery's Breath in the Flickering Glow

In twilight mist, where shadows play,
The faery's breath brightens the way.
With whispers soft, in moonlight swept,
Secrets of dreams are quietly kept.

Glimmers dance in the vibrant night,
A waltz of magic, pure delight.
Wings like gossamer, light as air,
They flit and twirl without a care.

Among the blooms, a gentle sigh,
From silver leaves, they catch the sky.
Each laugh a song, each tear a star,
Echoes of wishes from afar.

A candle's flicker, sparks aglow,
Boundless realms where wild dreams flow.
In a world that's spun from threads of gold,
A faery's tale is sweetly told.

Serenity Wrapped in Gilded Sparks

In quiet corners, soft and still,
A golden hush, the heart to fill.
With gentle hands, the stars unfold,
A tapestry of dreams in gold.

Each twinkling light, a whispered prayer,
A breath of peace fills the air.
With every spark, a story grows,
Of tender love that softly glows.

Wrapped in warmth, like a lover's embrace,
Time drifts slowly, a timeless grace.
Amidst the chaos, a tranquil shore,
Where hopes are born and spirits soar.

Beyond the reach of growing night,
Gilded sparks bring forth the light.
Serenity blooms, as dreams take flight,
In the sacred hush where hearts unite.

Kaleidoscope of the Dreamweaver's Flame

From dusk till dawn, the colors shift,
A dreamer's dance, the soul's sweet gift.
In visions bright, and shadows dear,
The weaver's flame draws all near.

With every thread, a tale unwinds,
Mysteries dance, the heart reminds.
A spectrum vast, a vibrant gleam,
Crafting worlds from threads of dream.

In every flicker, a story born,
Of wild adventures, and hearts reborn.
The kaleidoscope spins, bright and bold,
Weaving the dreams that never grow old.

Within the flame, imagination glows,
In spirals of thought, the magic flows.
Lost in the dance, we find our place,
In the weaver's spell, we embrace grace.

Celestial Whispers in Dusky Corners

In corners dim where shadows blend,
Celestial whispers gently send.
Soft murmurs float on starlit air,
Promises of hope, a tender glare.

A comet's trail, a fleeting dream,
Where stardust mingles with the gleam.
In hidden nooks, the silence hums,
A melody of what still comes.

Beneath the veil of the twilight sky,
Each breeze a secret, a gentle sigh.
In dusky realms, the night takes flight,
Wrapped in the glimmer of fading light.

The cosmos dances, a secret tune,
As wishes sail past the silver moon.
In whispered tales, new dreams ignite,
Celestial wonders guide our flight.

The Hearth of Gilded Whispers

In corners where the shadows play,
A fire whispers secrets of the day.
Gilded dreams float on the air,
Crafting visions, fragile and rare.

The embers dance with silken grace,
As memories shift in time's embrace.
Within this warmth, old tales unfold,
Of love and loss, of hearts of gold.

A flicker speaks of ages past,
Of fleeting moments, shadows cast.
With every crackle, stories weave,
In the hearth's glow, we dare believe.

When twilight deepens, the world grows still,
These whispers echo, a gentle thrill.
In twilight's arms, the shadows blend,
And dreams take flight, where all can mend.

So gather close, let hearts ignite,
In gilded whispers of the night.
For here we find, in every spark,
The tales that light the deepest dark.

Dances of Radiance and Shadow

A twilight waltz in silver beams,
Where light and dark entwine in dreams.
The moonlit glade, a stage so grand,
Where nimble spirits softly stand.

Swaying lightly on a breeze,
They merge in radiance with such ease.
In playful twirls, the shadows leap,
While whispers of the night become deep.

With every sway, a pulse we find,
In harmony of heart and mind.
The flicker of stars above our heads,
Guiding us along the paths we tread.

In this embrace of light and shade,
The dance of life is softly laid.
Let music rise in gentle streams,
In radiant flows, our spirit gleams.

So join the dance, both bright and dim,
In shadowed corners, let hopes brim.
For in each step, we learn to see,
The beauty held in mystery.

Ethereal Echoes in the Hearthshadow

Beneath the arch of looming night,
Ethereal echoes take their flight.
In the hearthshadow, dreams entwine,
Spun from whispers, soft and fine.

An ancient tune, like distant rain,
Calls forth the lost, to dance again.
Flickers of light in an endless sea,
Guide the wanderers, bold and free.

With every pulse, the shadows leap,
In corners where the memories sleep.
Stories linger on the woven air,
Glimmers of hope in the softest glare.

As time unfurls its silken thread,
The echoes wrap around our head.
In the hearthshadow, we find our way,
To brighter dawns that chase away gray.

So heed the call, let silence sing,
Endless echoes, the heart's true wing.
In every whisper, vast as the skies,
Lie dreams that sparkle like fireflies.

The Glow of Forgotten Legends

In twilight's grip, legends arise,
Bathed in the glow of starlit skies.
Forgotten tales, both dark and bright,
Whisper of magic, lost from sight.

With every ember's flickering light,
The olden stories take to flight.
Heroes bold with a fateful call,
Through verdant woods and shadowed hall.

A sword unsheathed, a maiden's song,
Resounded where the spirits throng.
The tapestry of fate weaves tight,
Leading us onward, into the night.

Each tale a thread in time's grand scheme,
Glowing softly in a wistful dream.
Let us gather, hearts intertwined,
In the glow of legends left behind.

So raise a toast to days of yore,
When light and dark would evermore
Dance together, in endless lore,
The glow of legends we adore.

Fantasies Carried by the Zephyr

Through whispering winds, the dreams take flight,
A dance of shadows in the soft moonlight.
With every sigh, the heart will sway,
To distant lands where the spirits play.

The clouds, like sailors, drift and roam,
Among the stars, they find a home.
In valleys deep where the fables grow,
There lies the magic we all long to know.

The zephyr speaks in a language rare,
Of lost adventures and secrets bare.
With gentle strength, it guides our way,
To realms of wonder, come what may.

So close your eyes and take a breath,
Embrace the whispers, put fear to rest.
For in the breeze so wild and free,
Are fantasies waiting for you and me.

As petals fall from the cherry tree,
They tell the stories of you and me.
With every gust, our dreams aspire,
To dance along on a thin wire.

Mirage of Dreams in Twilight's Hold

In twilight's grasp, where shadows blend,
The marigold sky, it seems to bend.
With hues of crimson, orange, and gold,
A mirage of dreams begins to unfold.

Across the fields where the night winds sigh,
Whispers of secrets float softly by.
In every corner, the starlight plays,
A canvas painted in twilight's gaze.

The lanterns flicker like distant flames,
Their glow a beacon for all our aims.
In soft-spoken words, the shadows call,
To weave our wishes, one and all.

And as the darkness begins to creep,
The promise of dreams lulls us to sleep.
In this twilight, our hearts entwine,
Creating magic that feels divine.

Where dreams and reality start to blend,
In twilight's hold, all sorrows mend.
A mirage of hope in the night's embrace,
Awaits the wanderers, a sacred space.

Aetherial Sparks in the Woodland

In the heart of the wood where the old trees sigh,
Aetherial sparks flicker, twinkle on high.
They dance through the branches, wild and free,
Unveiling stories for you and me.

With every step on the mossy floor,
The whispers of magic gently implore.
To pause, to listen, to feel the flow,
Of ancient wisdom, where soft winds blow.

The fae gather 'neath the silver glow,
Their laughter mingling with the night's soft flow.
In circles they weave their dainty thread,
Of tales spun where dreams are fed.

Hidden pathways call with a gentle hum,
To secret places where wild hearts come.
In the woodland's embrace, life's mysteries spark,
In the silence profound, we find our mark.

So roam through the dreams where the wild things play,
In the aetherial glow of the twilight's sway.
With open hearts and eyes anew,
The woodland whispers will guide us through.

Mysteries in the Shimmering Hearth

In the glow of the hearth, warmth we seek,
Mysteries linger, softly they speak.
With every flicker and crackling sound,
Tales of old families and legends abound.

A kettle whirls with secrets untold,
While shadows dance as the night grows bold.
In the amber light, stories take flight,
Unraveling dreams, both strange and bright.

The tapestry woven in flames so fair,
Comforts the weary, answers their prayer.
Through the night, hearts open wide,
In the shimmering hearth, where truths reside.

Like embers that spark with a timeless glow,
The wisdom of ages begins to flow.
Here in the stillness, we find our peace,
In mysteries whispered, our hearts release.

So gather 'round in the fire's embrace,
Through warmth and wonder, find your place.
For in this glow, life's magic breathes,
The mysteries of hearth, our souls it weaves.

A Tapestry Woven in Stardust

In the quiet of the night sky,
Stars spin tales of old,
Threads of magic weave gently,
A tapestry bright and bold.

Whispers float on the cool breeze,
Secrets carried from afar,
Each twinkle holds a promise,
Each gleam a guiding star.

Moonlight dances on rivers,
Casting shadows in the dark,
Nature's breath, a soft hum,
An enchanting, timeless spark.

Around the edges of silence,
Dreams take flight and soar,
Through the fabric of existence,
We find our hearts' core.

Wrapped in wonder and starlight,
We weave our fancies grand,
In this tapestry of stardust,
Together, hand in hand.

Fantasia Beneath the Flickering Glare

Underneath the lantern glow,
Fantasia weaves its spell,
Colors dance on whispered winds,
Magic cloaked in a shell.

Gentle laughter fills the air,
Echoes of a hidden cheer,
Every flicker tells a story,
Every shadow sings near.

Cloaked in shades of longing,
We wander paths unseen,
Where dreams meet the twilight,
In a world serene,

Through the gardens of the night,
Mysterious creatures roam,
Guided by the flicker,
In a place we can call home.

Among the stars and whispers,
We lose the weight of time,
In the heart of Fantasia,
Life becomes a rhyme.

Ethereal Sparks in the Faery Realm

Where the shadows softly shimmer,
Ethereal sparks ignite,
In the faery realm of wonder,
Magic dances in the light.

Petals glow with secrets sweet,
Moonbeams kiss the glade,
Every sigh a story spun,
In the twilight's jade.

Gentle wings take to the air,
Guided by a silver thread,
In this realm of faery dreams,
All fears and worries shed.

With a laugh, the night unfurls,
Mysteries swirl and weave,
In the heart of the enchanted,
We dare to believe.

Through the forest of enchantment,
We bask in the glow anew,
Ethereal sparks lead the way,
To worlds we never knew.

The Dance of Shimmering Spirits

In the twilight's gentle embrace,
Shimmering spirits take flight,
Through the weave of starry threads,
They whisper secrets of night.

Each movement a soft caress,
With grace they spin and twirl,
In a dance that knows no bounds,
Where time begins to unfurl.

Underneath the ancient trees,
Echoes linger and sway,
Rhythms of the universe,
In a grand ballet.

Hearts ignite in unison,
As laughter fills the air,
In this shimmering embrace,
Love breaks every despair.

As day bids farewell to night,
The spirits still remain,
In the dance of shimmering lights,
Our souls they gently gain.

Secrets of the Spellbound Ember

In the heart of the forest, a flicker ignites,
Whispers of magic in soft, gentle nights.
An ember that glows with a spark of the old,
Holds stories of wizards and secrets untold.

From shadows it beckons, with warmth it awaits,
Casting enchantments, unlocking the fates.
The leaves dance above, in a luminous haze,
As time drifts away in a mystical daze.

Each flicker a promise of power concealed,
For those who are brave and have courage revealed.
To seek out the magic, to hear the call,
Invoke the embers, let the shadows enthrall.

With hearts intertwined, we gather around,
To cherish the mysteries waiting unfound.
In the midst of the night, our spirits take flight,
As the secrets of fire shimmer ever bright.

So listen dear seekers, the fire's soft song,
Embrace the enchantment, where dreamers belong.
For within the glowing, the truth shall appear,
In the warmth of the ember, we cast away fear.

Luminous Threads in Twilight's Embrace

In the twilight's soft glow, new shadows arise,
Threads of silver weave through the deepening skies.
Each whisper of night cloaked in velvet's caress,
Unfolds hidden secrets in gentle finesse.

The stars start to twinkle, their stories unfold,
As dreams are stitched softly, with magic behold.
A tapestry woven of hopes and of fears,
In the silence of dusk, the heart's vision clears.

With each fleeting moment, our spirits align,
In the dance of the dusk, our fates intertwine.
The luminous threads pull us closer, they sing,
In harmony carved from the twilight of spring.

We walk through the shadows, our laughter takes flight,
Crafting enchanting tales beneath the moonlight.
Together we wander, where wishes are spun,
In the embrace of the night, we become one.

So revel in magic, let it guide your way,
Through the realm of the twilight, where dreams gently
sway.
With every soft whisper and mythical trace,
We find in the darkness our rightful place.

Echoes from the Mystic Fire

In the heart of the night, the firelight sways,
Echoes of stories in flickering rays.
Shadows are dancing, as whispers draw near,
Breath of the ages, both haunting and clear.

From the flames there arise the tales of the past,
Of courage and magic that ever shall last.
Beneath the warm glow, we gather around,
In the hush of the night, where memories abound.

Each crackle a promise, each spark a new hope,
Guiding the lost on their ephemeral slope.
Timeless and endless, the stories we weave,
In the warmth of the fire, our hearts learn to believe.

As embers take flight, like dreams on the wing,
We cherish the warmth that the mystic fires bring.
In the rhythm and pulse of the flame's gentle dance,
We find our connection, a magical chance.

So gather ye round, let the night draw you close,
In the flicker of embers, our spirits engross.
For echoes of magic will linger and play,
In the glow of the fire, we shall find our way.

Shadows Dancing in Gossamer Light

In twilight's embrace, the shadows do sway,
Dancing on moonbeams, they frolic and play.
Gossamer threads spin the dark into grace,
Painting the night with a silvery trace.

With each gentle movement, the secrets unfold,
Whispers of magic in stories retold.
Weaving through silence, the shadows conspire,
To ignite the embers of long-hidden fire.

In the stillness of night, our hearts come alive,
As shadows are sculptors, our dreams they derive.
An invitation to journey beyond,
Where wonders abound and the spirit grows fond.

So let us embrace the enchantment around,
In the depth of the night, where mysteries abound.
Through gossamer light and in shadows we glide,
In the dance of our dreams, we find love as our guide.

Embrace the soft whispers, the magic in view,
For shadows hold secrets and pathways anew.
Together we wander through landscapes of night,
In the truth of our hearts and the glow of the light.

Glimmers of Ethereal Dreams

In twilight's veil, where shadows play,
A whisper calls from far away,
A flicker of hope in starlit skies,
Where magic dances, and longing lies.

Beneath the boughs of ancient trees,
The moonlight weaves through silver leaves,
A tapestry of dreams unfurled,
In the embrace of a hidden world.

With every breath, a spirit sighs,
The laughter held in magic's eyes,
In the quiet night, the heart takes flight,
To chase the stars, the wishes bright.

Glimmers of hope like fireflies,
Illuminate the darkest skies,
Guiding the lost on paths anew,
In the realm where dreams come true.

So close your eyes and drift away,
To lands where night meets budding day,
With open hearts, let wishes gleam,
In the glow of ethereal dream.

Whispers Through the Enchanted Flames

In the hearth where embers glow,
Ancient tales begin to flow,
The crackling fire spills its charm,
Wrapping all in a warm, sweet balm.

Each spark that leaps like secrets told,
Weaves through the night in whispers bold,
Echoes of magic, shadows cast,
Of times long gone and dreams amassed.

Flames flicker like a lover's gaze,
Enchanting hearts in a fiery haze,
With stories sung by the night's soft breath,
Carrying echoes beyond the death.

Listen closely to the crackling sound,
For hidden truths in flames are found,
A mirror of hopes, of fears unclaimed,
In embers' dance, forever framed.

So gather 'round, let your spirits soar,
As whispers through the flames implore,
In the warmth of night, lose all your cares,
And find the magic in whispered prayers.

Illusions in the Sylvan Glow

In the forest rich with life and sound,
Where secrets of the earth abound,
A path emerges, soft and low,
Leading forth to the sylvan glow.

The leaves above, a vibrant hue,
Bathe all beneath in morning dew,
While whispers linger in fragrant air,
A tapestry of dreams laid bare.

Creatures flit with nimble grace,
In dappled light, they find their place,
Each rustle speaks of tales untold,
In a realm where magic unfolds.

With every step, enchantment grows,
Through fragrant blooms and hidden foes,
Illusions swirl like a gentle breeze,
Woven softly through the trees.

So wander forth where shadows play,
Embrace the life in wild array,
For in this realm where spirits flow,
You'll find your heart in sylvan glow.

Reflections of Moonlit Fantasies

Beneath the moon's soft, silver light,
Fairy tales take their gentle flight,
As shadows dance on the quiet ground,
In dreams where hope and love are found.

The stars above weave stories bright,
Illuminating the velvet night,
Each glimmer is a wish set free,
In the land of sweet reverie.

The nightingale sings of lore untold,
Of whispered secrets and hearts so bold,
As silver beams on water play,
Casting wishes that drift away.

In the cool embrace of evening's grace,
Every heartbeat finds its place,
Reflections of dreams begin to bloom,
In the gentle hush of midnight's room.

So linger here in the soft moon's glow,
Where fantasies flourish and wonders flow,
Embrace the mystique of twilight's dance,
In a world alive with dreamlike chance.

Chasing the Light of a Thousand Stars

In the velvet sky, dreams arise,
Whispers of night where magic lies.
Each twinkle bright, a story spun,
As we chase the light, reaching the sun.

Through shadows thick, we weave our fate,
Every heartbeat echoes, never late.
With wishes cast, like paper planes,
We'll dance on starlight, breaking chains.

Across the fields where wishes roam,
We stoke the flames, find a home.
Each spark ignites, our hearts combine,
In the starlit glow, our souls entwine.

Nebulas whisper their tender songs,
In cosmic dreams, where we belong.
The night unfolds, a canvas bright,
Painting our journey with endless light.

Join me, dear friend, into the sky,
We'll catch a comet, watch it fly.
With every glance, the galaxies call,
In this endless dance, we rise, we fall.

The Incandescent Glow of Sprite Wings

In a forest deep, where secrets dwell,
Sprite wings shimmer with a magic spell.
Glowing bright in the moonlight's grace,
They spin and twirl, a fluid race.

Through leaves they flit, a delicate hum,
Each flicker of light, a vibrant drum.
They whisper tales of the ancient wise,
In the glow of the night, their laughter flies.

Softly they gather, a luminous fleet,
With shimmering hues, they dance on repeat.
The air thick with wonder, every breath,
In their incandescent glow, life feels blessed.

Beneath the starlight, they weave a dream,
In a world painted by their gleaming beam.
With every flutter, a spell ignite,
Sprite wings beckon to the heart's delight.

Join the dance under silvery skies,
Let your spirit soar, let your soul rise.
In the magic found, in each gentle wing,
Awaken the wonders, the joy they bring.

Shadows Dancing with Luminescence

In twilight's embrace, shadows grow long,
Whispers of night weave a haunting song.
Dancing notes blend, a silken haze,
As shadows twirl in a starry maze.

Underneath stars, they sway and glide,
In a waltz of mystery, they cannot hide.
With every flicker, luminescence glows,
A dance of whispers, where no one knows.

Echoes of laughter in the cool night air,
Drawn to the light, a enchanting snare.
Together they spin, a breathtaking sight,
Shadows and glimmer, intertwined in flight.

A brush of magic at the close of day,
With each gentle turn, they lead the way.
Through realms of wonder, where dreams reside,
Shadows dancing, with light as their guide.

So let your spirit join in the play,
Find solace and peace in the night's ballet.
In the shimmer and sway, leave fears behind,
In this dance of shadows, true magic you'll find.

Feathered Dreams in Tapestry Light

In a realm where dreams take flight,
Feathers whisper in the soft twilight.
A tapestry woven of colors bright,
Each thread a story, a heart's delight.

Through the glade, they drift and soar,
Carrying wishes from shore to shore.
With every feather, a promise made,
In the twilight's glow, fears start to fade.

Underneath branches, secrets unfold,
In the embrace of night, the brave and bold.
They weave through the stars, a soft serenade,
In the tapestry light, dreams never fade.

Join the enchantment, let your heart sing,
In feathered dreams, feel the magic ring.
Each flutter a wish that rides the wind,
In this wondrous world, our spirits rescind.

So lift up your heart, let your dreams ignite,
In the warmth of the stars, embrace the night.
For in every feather, a journey takes flight,
In the tapestry light, we shine ever bright.

Embers of Magic in the Woodland Hearth

In the hush of night, whispers dance,
Leaves like secrets under the moon's glance,
Flames crackle softly, shadows take flight,
Beneath the stars, the embers ignite.

Creatures of wonder peek through the trees,
Their hearts ablaze with ancient decrees,
Woven in twilight, a tapestry spun,
Binding the dreamers, the magic begun.

The air is thick with stories untold,
Of heroes and journeys, both brave and bold,
In each flicker of fire, a wisdom resides,
A tapestry rich where fantasy hides.

Gathered together, a feast of the mind,
Adventures await in the world we will find,
In the glow of the hearth, we'll forge a new tale,
As the night wraps around us, a silken veil.

So lift your cups high, let laughter take wing,
In the woodland's embrace, our spirits will sing,
For here in this moment, forever we'll be,
In the embers of magic, eternally free.

A Palette of Dreams and Dreams Untold

In fields of color, the dreams take flight,
Brushstrokes of hope painted bold in the night,
Whispers of wishes burst forth from the heart,
Each hue a reminder, we're never apart.

With shades of longing, the canvas unveils,
A symphony vibrant, where silence prevails,
The laughter of starlight, a luminous tune,
Enveloping us in the embrace of the moon.

From azure to crimson, the palette declares,
A dance of emotions, unspoken affairs,
In slumbers we wander, where fantasies dwell,
In a world painted brightly, where all is well.

Each dream is a journey in splashes of time,
A landscape of wonder, a rhythm, a rhyme,
As we hold onto visions that shimmer and glide,
In the heart of our dreams, we can safely confide.

So let the colors swirl, let the daylight unroll,
For each stroke tells stories that touch the soul,
Together we'll wander, with purpose and grace,
In a palette of dreams, we'll find our true place.

Enchantment in the Cradle of Light

In the cradle of dawn where the shadows dissolve,
Mysteries shimmer, the world starts to evolve,
Petals unfurling to greet the new day,
As dawn's gentle fingers weave light in the gray.

The air is aglow with a soft, golden hue,
Whispers of magic in everything new,
The laughter of sunlight plays hide and seek,
Enchantment surrounds us; it's vibrant, unique.

In gardens of wonder where fairies might roam,
The heart of each blossom invites you back home,
Each fluttering leaf carries stories from long,
Echoes of chorus in nature's sweet song.

Embrace the crescendo, the symphony calls,
In the cradle of light, enchantment enthralls,
With each step we take, let excitement ignite,
In the dance of the day, we'll find our delight.

For the world is a canvas, alive with intent,
A masterpiece waiting, where dreams are unbent,
In the cradle of light, let our spirits take flight,
Together we'll cherish this magical sight.

Secrets of the Sylvan Sanctuary

In whispers soft, the forest sighs,
Where sunlight dances, truth belies.
With every leaf a tale untold,
The secrets lie in shadows bold.

Beneath the boughs, the spirits dwell,
In hidden glades, a magic swell.
A flicker here, a shimmer bright,
They weave their dreams, in silver light.

The ancient trees, they guard the lore,
Of all the worlds that came before.
Their roots, they cradle time and space,
In nature's arms, a warm embrace.

With every breeze, the whispers call,
A melody that bards install.
In harmony, the woodlands sing,
The joy and sorrow that they bring.

So pause awhile, in tranquil shade,
Let secrets lie, and fears evade.
For in the sylvan sanctuary's heart,
The magic lives, it won't depart.

Ethereal Flickers at Dusk

The twilight fades, the stars take flight,
In hues of gold, the coming night.
A shimmer glows, like whispered dreams,
And dancing light through starlit beams.

In corners dark, where shadows play,
Ethereal flickers mark the way.
The fireflies weave their fleeting art,
With every pulse, a beating heart.

The gentle night, it wraps us tight,
In threads of peace, in cloak of night.
A symphony of sounds unfolds,
As magic in the dusk beholds.

Across the sky, a canvas bright,
Where moonbeams kiss the earth goodnight.
A velvet hush consumes the air,
In clarity, we linger there.

So chase the flickers, let them guide,
Through tranquil paths, the stars abide.
In every blink, a wonder waits,
Unraveling the night's true fates.

Lullabies of the Moonlit Grove

Beneath the moon, the shadows sway,
As night unveils the fading day.
In silvered light, the branches hum,
A lullaby that bids us come.

The cool grass beckons, soft and sweet,
Where dreams and waking worlds may meet.
A serenade of rustling leaves,
As nature's heart together weaves.

Each note a whisper, rich and deep,
That calls the weary world to sleep.
A gentle touch, a soothing balm,
To weave the night in peaceful calm.

And in the grove, the spirits glide,
With every breeze, their laughter bides.
In hidden depths, their secrets dwell,
In ancient tales, they weave a spell.

So linger long, in this embrace,
Let moonbeams cast their tender grace.
For in this grove, we find our peace,
In lullabies that never cease.

Threads of Enchantment and Light

In woven dreams, the magic sings,
A tapestry of cherished things.
With threads of gold, the fable spools,
Through hearts of wizards, wise as fools.

Embroidered stars in sky's embrace,
They twinkle down with gentle grace.
Each starlit path, a story spun,
Of battles lost and battles won.

Through shadows deep and rivers wide,
The threads of fate, they intertwine.
In every twist, a tale unfolds,
Of whispered dreams and treasures gold.

In light's warm glow, the secrets hide,
In every nook, where joys abide.
With every stitch, the magic grows,
In timeless realms, where wonder flows.

So take a thread, let's weave our tale,
With colors bright that never pale.
In splendor vast, we'll find our flight,
In threads of enchantment and light.

Breaths of the Forgotten Fable

In the shadows of olden days,
Where whispers weave through emerald haze,
A tale unfolds in gentle sighs,
With echoes soft as twilight flies.

Once danced the dreams, now lost in time,
In secret glades where fairies rhyme,
A melody that beckons slow,
Of laughter bright and sorrows low.

Through tangled woods, the secrets creep,
Where willows weep and silence keep,
With every breath, the fable stirs,
Awakening heart, the wonder occurs.

Beneath the moon's embrace so pale,
The stories, rich as starlit veil,
With every breath, the past arrives,
And in that moment, magic thrives.

So listen close, let echoes guide,
Through time's embrace, forever wide,
The fable breathes, a gentle lore,
In hearts of those who seek for more.

Splendor Woven in Celestial Threads

In the loom of night, the stars align,
Crafting dreams from threads divine,
Each glimmer weaves a tale untold,
In silver patterns, brave and bold.

The cosmos hums a sacred tune,
With whispers soft from sun and moon,
A tapestry of hopes and fears,
Embroidered deep with ancient tears.

In every stitch, a spark of light,
Guiding souls through velvet night,
With destinies that intertwine,
In splendor's grace, forever shine.

Beneath the arch of twilight's glow,
The wonders of the heavens flow,
Each heartbeat syncs with starlit dance,
In cosmic threads, we find our chance.

So let your spirit soar and drift,
In splendor woven, discover gift,
For every dream held close inside,
Is part of this celestial ride.

Celestial Revelations Amidst the Glimmers

In the silence of the asking night,
Revelations sparkle, soft and bright,
The cosmos spills its stardust dreams,
In fragments of the light that gleams.

Each twinkling star, a question posed,
In shadowed realms where hope is closed,
Yet seekers find a path to grace,
With every glance to heaven's face.

The universe, a tapestry vast,
With secrets of the future past,
As comets blaze across the sky,
We grasp at truths and learn to fly.

In whispers shared, connections grow,
Through cosmic threads we learn to know,
That all is woven, all is one,
Beneath the watchful gaze of sun.

So let your heart embrace the night,
For in the dark, you'll find the light,
In celestial wonders, revelations bloom,
A journey cherished, amidst the gloom.

Dreams Glistening in Sylvan Fire

In the heart of woods where shadows dance,
Dreams awaken, in a trance,
With whispers soft like evening's tide,
In sylvan fire, our hopes abide.

The embers glow with stories old,
Of brave adventures, wonders bold,
Each flicker sparks the mind's delight,
Beneath the stars, in velvet night.

As leaves of gold in breezes twirl,
In this enchanted, mystic whirl,
The twilight hums a haunting song,
Where dreams and nature both belong.

The woodland spirits guard the flame,
With gentle grace, they call your name,
Through rustling leaves and shadows cast,
Embrace the moments, let them last.

So gather 'round the sylvan glow,
Where dreams ignite, and spirits flow,
For in this realm, so pure, so bright,
We weave our dreams into the night.

Bubbles of Light in Fairy Pools

In pools where whispers softly gleam,
Bubbles rise like forgotten dreams.
Dancing under the moon's embrace,
Light twinkles bright in this secret place.

Water sprites with laughter ring,
Their joyous songs make the night sing.
Rippling shadows, a spectral sight,
Echo secrets of pure delight.

With touches shy of softest glow,
The fae weave tales only they know.
Each bubble bursts with a wish in store,
A promise made forevermore.

The stars above cast their watchful gaze,
On laughter carved in moonlit haze.
With each ripple, a story unfolds,
In fairy pools where silence holds.

So wander near where the magic flows,
And find the joy that the heart bestows.
For in this realm where the pure hearts dwell,
Bubbles of light cast their timeless spell.

The Heartbeat of Enchanted Flames

In the hearth where shadows play,
Enchanted flames dance night and day.
With crackling whispers, they ignite,
The darkest corners, bringing light.

Glimmers twirl with a fierce embrace,
As warmth envelops the entire space.
The heartbeat of magic in every spark,
Illuminating dreams that live in the dark.

With stories sung of olden lore,
The flames recount what came before.
Each flicker tells of battles won,
In the glow of the embers, hopes are spun.

So gather 'round the fire's heart,
Feel its rhythm, let it impart.
Lessons woven with each gentle sway,
In enchanted flames, all fears decay.

With every flame, a wish takes flight,
Echoing tales in the warm moonlight.
In this glow, let the world unwind,
For the heartbeat of flames, is love entwined.

Veils of Luster in the Glade

In the glade where secrets lie,
Veils of luster catch the eye.
Whispers weave through emerald boughs,
Nature's wonders take their vows.

From silver dew on petals bright,
To dancing patterns in soft twilight.
Gossamer threads flutter and sway,
Softly guiding the wanderer's way.

Crickets sing of twilight's grace,
While shadows twirl in an ancient space.
Fae flit by with laughter light,
In the glade, all hearts take flight.

Bathed in hues of dusk and dawn,
The luster breathes, never fully gone.
For with each breath of the night air,
The glade holds magic, timeless and rare.

So pause in wonder, let silence claim,
The treasure found in nature's name.
For veils of luster, a soft refrain,
In this enchanted glade, love will remain.

Secrets Shared by the Flickering Fire

By the flickering fire, secrets grow,
Stories whispered in the glowing flow.
Shadows dance on the earthen floor,
As the night unveils what hearts adore.

Ghosts of memory wander near,
As laughter mingles with whispered fear.
Each crackle of wood holds a past,
In the warmth of the fire, moments last.

The flames weave tales of joy and pain,
Binding souls with a golden chain.
In the light, both shadows and song,
All are welcome; all belong.

So lean in close, let your heart bare,
For in the fire, love's essence is rare.
With each flicker, a truth is shared,
In the warmth of the flame, no heart is scared.

To the flickering fire, we draw nigh,
In its glow, every secret can fly.
A gathering place, where stories inspire,
Is the beauty found by the flickering fire.

Chasing Wisps of Celestial Color

In twilight's glow, the stars arise,
Chasing dreams that paint the skies.
Whispers of wonder, soft and sweet,
Dancing shadows with nimble feet.

Through fields of stardust, we will roam,
Seeking colors that feel like home.
Each flicker brings a tale untold,
A secret world of shades of gold.

The moon beams bright on twilight's stage,
Unraveling mysteries from each page.
With every step, horizons shift,
In a galaxy where dreams uplift.

The night unfolds its velvet cloak,
In silence, ancient songs are woke.
Daring hearts, take flight, take chance,
Chasing wisps in a twilight dance.

So come, dear friend, and take my hand,
We'll wander deep through this dreamland.
With every moment, sparks ignite,
Chasing colors through the night.

Realm of Flickering Enchantment

In the wood, where secrets dwell,
A realm of magic casts its spell.
Flickering lights in soft embrace,
Guide the lost to a safe place.

Beneath the boughs, soft whispers hum,
Echoes of joy, a gentle strum.
In this haven, shadows play,
Transforming dusk into the day.

A flicker here, a glimmer there,
Dreams entwined in the cool night air.
Fireflies dance in joyous flight,
Painting stories in the night.

The winds will tell of paths well-tread,
Of lovers lost, of stories read.
In every corner, magic spins,
With each new dawn, the journey begins.

So linger long in twilight's glow,
Embrace the charms the night will show.
In this realm where wonders gleam,
Life's an ever-changing dream.

The Hearth's Glowing Reverie

By the hearth, where warmth does flow,
Stories flicker in the embers' glow.
With every crackle, tales unfold,
Of heart's desires, both young and old.

A tapestry of voices weave,
Whispers of those who still believe.
Nostalgia dances in the light,
As shadows gather close at night.

In the comfort of this sacred space,
Time stands still in a warm embrace.
Words take flight in a gentle stream,
Filling hearts with hope and dream.

Moments cherished, laughter shared,
In the glowing warmth, we're unprepared.
For every heartbeat, joy ignites,
In the hearth's glowing, tender sights.

So draw near, let your spirits soar,
With every story, we'll call for more.
In the flicker, the heart will see,
A glowing reverie, wild and free.

Enchanted Light in the Heart of the Wood

In the heart of the wood, where silence sings,
Enchanted light weaves a tapestry of things.
Golden beams through the leaves cascade,
Creating shadows, a playful charade.

Creatures stir in twilight's hush,
In this garden, dreams softly rush.
A flicker, a rustle, a call from afar,
Guiding lost souls like a bright, guiding star.

Every step reveals hidden lore,
Ancient echoes from a forgotten shore.
Wonders blossom in emerald glades,
As whispers of magic in twilight parades.

The trees stand tall, with arms outstretched,
Guardians of secrets, lovingly etched.
In this sanctuary, hope is reborn,
By enchanted light at the breaking dawn.

So venture deep, where the heart feels free,
Let the wood's embrace whisper to thee.
In the softest glow, find what you seek,
Enchanted light, tender yet meek.

Whimsy Born of Fostered Firelight

In the heart of twilight's gleam,
Flickering flames dance and dream,
Whispers rise on gentle sighs,
As secrets twine 'neath starlit skies.

Puppeteers of night they sing,
Casting spells with each soft fling,
Cloaked in mystery, shadows sway,
Where fantasy and wishes play.

Firelight glows with tales untold,
Of creatures bright and hearts of gold,
A tapestry of dreams unspun,
In the warm embrace of night begun.

Gather 'round, let stories flow,
Fostered flames in a radiant show,
With each spark, a wish takes flight,
In the whimsy born of firelight.

So raise your cups, let laughter soar,
As embers dance forevermore,
In the realm where wishes twine,
Underneath this sky divine.

Threads of Light in the Starlit Woods

In the woods where shadows weave,
Threads of light we can believe,
Whispers twist in the cool night air,
Painting dreams beyond compare.

The moonlit path, a silver thread,
Guides our steps as we tread,
Elusive phantoms dart and play,
In the hushed embrace of the day.

Softly glows the fae's delight,
Casting echoes in the night,
Glimmers dance in leafy boughs,
Where magic blooms and time allows.

With every step, enchantments bloom,
In this sacred, starlit room,
Life unfurls in gentle grace,
Among the shadows, find our place.

A tapestry of hope and gleam,
Together we shall weave and dream,
In the woods, beneath the skies,
Where threads of light will always rise.

Spirals of Dreamscapes in the Glow

In the depths of midnight's song,
Dreamscapes spiral, wild and strong,
Colors swirl in liquid night,
Whirling visions, pure delight.

Gossamer paths thread through the dark,
Each twinkle forms a glowing spark,
Where echoes of our wishes flow,
In a dance of light and shadow.

Fleeting moments caught in air,
A world of wonder waits us there,
Through spirals of the wide unknown,
To realms of magic, we have grown.

In this glow, all fears shall fade,
As we follow where hopes parade,
Galaxies within each thought,
With every dream, our souls are caught.

So let us twirl in the embrace,
Of dreamscapes filled with timeless grace,
In spirals bright, we shall explore,
The universe forevermore.

The Lightweaver's Quilt of Dreams

In twilight's hush, the weaver starts,
Stitching threads of wandering hearts,
A quilt of dreams from dusk till dawn,
Where whispers of the night are drawn.

Each patch a story, each seam a sigh,
Wrapped in magic, soaring high,
Patterns woven with tales of old,
In silver light and stardust bold.

The moon's soft glow, a guiding light,
Embroidered visions take their flight,
Within the fibers, secrets swirl,
As the night reveals its precious pearl.

Upon this quilt, our dreams shall stand,
With love and hope, a gentle hand,
Intertwined, our fates aligned,
In every thread, our stories bind.

So gather close, embrace the weave,
In twilight's quilt, we dare believe,
With every stitch, a future gleams,
In the lightweaver's quilt of dreams.

Hearthlight of Whimsy and Wonder

In the glow of the hearth, dreams take flight,
Elves and fairies dance through the night.
Laughter weaves with magic spun,
A tapestry bright, where joy has begun.

Whispers of stories, old and new,
Mingle with shadows and soft dew.
Charmed by the flicker, hearts entwine,
In the warmth of wonder, sweet as wine.

The crackle of wood sings ancient lore,
Of hidden realms we all adore.
Each ember a star, burning in time,
A rhythm of life, a gentle rhyme.

Underneath the mantle, secrets lay,
In the hearthlight's glow, they softly sway.
With every gaze, our spirits soar,
Bound by the hearth, forevermore.

Flickering Feels of Nature's Charm

In the glade where wildflowers sway,
The sunbeams dance both bright and gay.
Nature's whispers guide the way,
Where every heart learns how to play.

Leaves rustle gently, secrets shared,
All creatures pause, intently paired.
A symphony sings in joyful tones,
A harmony deep in nature's bones.

Beneath the boughs, we find our peace,
In every breeze, our worries cease.
Moss-clad stones hold stories old,
In shades of green, like tales retold.

The river murmurs, a soothing guide,
While fireflies twinkle, side by side.
With each step forward, we're set free,
In this enchanted realm, just you and me.

Radiant Tales from the Heartwood

In the heartwood deep, where wonders lie,
Ancient oaks stretch to the sky.
Branches weave tales of days gone past,
Whispers of magic that ever last.

With roots entwined, the stories grow,
Of hidden gardens and moonlit glow.
A cradle of life, of joy and strife,
Where every whisper tells of life.

Saplings reach for the sky so wide,
While shadows of wisdom beneath abide.
Each ring of a tree holds secrets vast,
In radiant tales, firm yet fast.

The forest breathes with a timeless grace,
In every corner, a sacred space.
As we wander the paths, our spirits swell,
In the heartwood deep, our stories dwell.

Firelight Dances of the Enchanted Few

By the firelight's glow, spirits arise,
Twinkling as stars in enchanting skies.
With each flicker, old memories tell,
Of journeys taken, of magic's spell.

In shadows that waltz, we find our place,
Together we weave dreams, full of grace.
The heat of the flames warms our hearts true,
In these moments, all worlds feel new.

Stories spin forth in the crackling air,
Of bravery bold and love laid bare.
Captured in laughter, in wisdom's embrace,
The firelight dances, soft as lace.

With each heartbeat, we savor the night,
Lost in the magic, in love's gentle light.
For those who gather, the circle makes,
A bond unbroken, where every heart aches.

A Symphony of Glittering Spirits

In twilight's embrace, whispers take flight,
Dancing on breezes, soft as the night.
They weave through the stars, a silvery thread,
Carrying secrets of dreams yet unsaid.

With laughter like chimes, they play their sweet tune,
Drawing hearts closer beneath the pale moon.
Each note a reminder of paths we've not trod,
A symphony sung in the voice of the gods.

They shimmer like diamonds in shadows they cast,
Binding the present with echoes of past.
In the stillness, their magic begins to ignite,
Illuminating darkness with pure, gentle light.

With each fleeting moment, they sparkle and sway,
Inviting us deeper, where wonders hold sway.
Come dance with the spirits, under skies vast and bright,
For in their sweet chorus, we find pure delight.

So let us unite in this cosmic ballet,
Embracing the music that calls us to play.
With hearts intertwined, as we follow their flight,
We'll weave our own symphony, shining with light.

Fables Carved in Shivering Light

In the hush of the moonlight, stories unfold,
Whispers of fables as ancient as gold.
They flicker and shimmer, like sparks in the dark,
Carving their truths with a delicate mark.

With each breath of the night, legends take form,
Woven in elegance, they weather the storm.
Tales of the brave, of love, and of loss,
In the glow of their fire, hearts dare to cross.

The shadows may tremble, yet courage stands tall,
As echoes of laughter break through the night's thrall.
For each story told in the softest of light,
Holds the warmth and the chill of life's endless fight.

Embers of memories dance in the air,
Fables entwined with a thread of despair.
Yet hope sparkles brightly, igniting our sight,
As we gather the tales carved in shivering light.

So gather around as the night whispers low,
Listen to fables through twilight's soft glow.
For in every heart, a story takes flight,
Carved into time, forever in sight.

The Dance of Gilded Shadows

In the still of the dusk, shadows begin to rise,
Gilded with starlight, they shimmer and guise.
They swirl and they twirl in a magical trance,
Inviting the dreamers to join in their dance.

With laughter like bells, they echo through trees,
Whispering secrets in the soft evening breeze.
Each movement a story, each leap a refrain,
In the heart of the night, they weave joy through pain.

The moon casts her gaze on this waltz of delight,
As shadows enchant with their shimmering flight.
They beckon the weary to shed their despair,
And lose themselves fully in the magic they bear.

Together they take on a life of their own,
Each flicker a promise of dreams yet unknown.
In the dim glow, fears and worries dissolve,
As the dance of the shadows begins to evolve.

So let go of burdens, and follow their call,
For the dance of gilded shadows awaits us all.
In the tapestry woven by night's tender arms,
We'll find hidden beauty in darkness that charms.

Glistening Memories Beneath the Stars

Beneath the vast canvas of a starry night,
Glistening memories glitter, sparkling bright.
They whisper of laughter, of moments gone by,
Amongst the constellations, they twinkle and sigh.

Each star holds a story, a glimpse from the past,
A treasure of feelings, forever to last.
In the gentle embrace of the night's loving glow,
We gather the glimmers of all that we know.

With each silver flicker, a heartbeat of time,
Resonates softly, a delicate chime.
Reliving the joy, the heartache, the mirth,
As we trace our own stories, etched deep in the earth.

So look to the heavens, where dreams come alive,
In the dance of the stardust, our memories thrive.
For every bright glint in the dark velvet sea,
Is a part of our journey, of you and of me.

With hearts wide open, beneath the night's shawl,
We cherish the glistening, the rise and the fall.
In memories whispered, forever we find,
The magic of moments, eternally kind.

Chimerical Firelight on the Edge of Dreams

In the twilight's gentle glow,
Shadows dance and secrets flow.
Figures flicker in the mist,
A world where dreams and hopes exist.

Whispers weave through autumn leaves,
Each heart beats, and each one grieves.
Magic sings in whispered tones,
In firelight, we find our homes.

Beneath the stars, the dreamers sigh,
As fireflies twinkle in the sky.
With every flicker, fantasies weave,
In night's embrace, we dare believe.

Chimeras born of night and day,
Guide us softly on our way.
The edge of dreams, where wishes spark,
In burning light, we find the dark.

So let us gather, hearts afire,
Chasing dreams that never tire.
For in this place, where moments gleam,
We hold the threads of every dream.

Whispers of Iridescent Dreams

In the hush of emerald leaves,
Moonlight glimmers, softly weaves.
Whispers float on evening air,
A tapestry of wishes rare.

Each note of night, a secret told,
In shimmering hues of silver and gold.
With every breath, the magic hums,
As dawn awakens, gently comes.

Reflections dance in twilight's grasp,
A world of wonders held so fast.
Between the dreams, the story lies,
Where every heart learns to rise.

Iridescent visions shine,
In every thread, a hint divine.
Through realms of hope, we'll glide and sway,
In whispers soft, we find our way.

So dare to dream, and let it flow,
In every heart, let magic grow.
For in the night, our souls shall gleam,
Awake to life, and live the dream.

Luminous Secrets Beneath the Canopy

Beneath the branches, shadows play,
Where whispers hide and secrets stay.
The moonlit glow ignites the leaves,
In nature's arms, the heart believes.

Luminous beams of silver light,
Guide us through the enchanted night.
Fragrant blooms and breezes tune,
A symphony beneath the moon.

In the stillness, magic stirs,
As ancient dreams become a blur.
Softly woven tales unfold,
In whispers shared, and stories told.

Secrets linger in the air,
Wrap us gently in their care.
With every step, a path revealed,
In nature's hold, our fate is sealed.

So let the woods embrace our souls,
As heartbeats steady, love consoles.
For in this place, where shadows dance,
We find the light, we take a chance.

Glimmers in the Enchanted Flame

In the hearth, the embers glow,
A tale unfolds, as shadows grow.
Glimmers spark in flames alive,
Where olden myths and dreams arrive.

Whispers twirl in flickering light,
Inviting all to take their flight.
Through ash and smoke, the visions rise,
In every spark, a world defies.

The dance of fire, a timeless lore,
Binding hearts forevermore.
With every flick, a story spins,
In the warmth, our journey begins.

As the night weaves its gentle spell,
In glowing warmth, we find our dwell.
Each glimmer holds a dream untold,
In the flames, our spirits bold.

So gather 'round, and let hearts flame,
For in this night, we'll stake our claim.
In enchanted light, our souls will soar,
A dance of dreams, forevermore.

Embers Singing in the Night

In the hush of the twilight sky,
Fires flicker and softly sigh.
The shadows dance, they weave and spin,
Whispers echo where dreams begin.

Stars awaken, their twinkle bright,
Guiding souls through velvet night.
With every spark, tales come alive,
As hearts unburdened gently strive.

A warmth that pulses, a radiant glow,
Secrets shared, for only they know.
Old stories told by flickering light,
Embers singing, a timeless sight.

In this moment, the world feels near,
Each laughter, each sigh, crystal clear.
Underneath the crescent moon's smile,
We linger here for just a while.

To chase the dawn is to miss the best,
In fireside chats, we're truly blessed.
So gather close, let the magic ignite,
For embers sing in the quiet night.

Crystalline Whispers in the Glade

In the heart of the verdant glade,
Where sunlight dappled the cool cascade.
Crystal whispers drift through the trees,
Carried softly on the gentle breeze.

Glistening leaves in the morning light,
Each drop of dew a jewel so bright.
Nature's song, a sacred tune,
Echoes sweetly beneath the moon.

Frogs croak softly, the brook hums low,
In this tranquil realm, wonders grow.
With every step, the magic unfolds,
In crystalline air, tender and bold.

The wildflowers sway, a tapestry spun,
Dancing in rhythm, one by one.
In hidden corners, secrets are kept,
Where crystalline whispers have quietly crept.

So linger a moment, breathe in the peace,
Let worries and fears slowly cease.
In the glade's embrace, we find our place,
Where crystalline whispers forever grace.

Light Drifting Through the Mystic Veil

In the realm where the shadows dwell,
Light weaves through a mystic spell.
A dazzle of colors, pure and bright,
As dawn breaks free from the grips of night.

Softly it flutters, a dancer divine,
In hidden corners, its essence entwines.
Each ray a promise, each hue a song,
Guiding our hearts where we belong.

Through gossamer threads, life's patterns unfold,
In a shimmering tapestry, stories told.
With every flicker, a vision calls,
Illuminating the silent halls.

In the embrace of the morning's light,
Cornflower blue and golden white.
For in this glow, we cease to roam,
Finding within a place called home.

So gather the moments, let them ignite,
As light drifts softly through the mystic night.
With hearts wide open, we shall embrace,
The magic of light in this enchanted space.

The Embrace of Fabled Illumination

Among the tales of ages past,
Fabled dreams in shadows cast.
Illumination beckons near,
A gentle warmth, a voice we hear.

In whispered woods where legends sleep,
The secrets of time are ours to keep.
With every ray that sparkles bright,
We weave our hopes in the cloak of night.

Hallucinations of light and lore,
Invite us to explore once more.
As ancient songs begin to play,
In our hearts, forever stay.

The dance of fate, a guiding muse,
Fabled illumination we choose.
Through brilliance shared beneath the stars,
We find connection, no distance far.

So take my hand, let shadows fade,
In the embrace of dreams we've made.
Through radiant realms, we'll intertwine,
As fabled stories become divine.

Journeys Through Beloved Phosphors

Through starlit paths, the wanderers roam,
In search of whispers, where shadows comb.
Each footstep glimmers with hope anew,
Guiding lost souls to skies so blue.

In twilight's embrace, old tales unfold,
Of courage and magic, of hearts made bold.
With phosphor glows that dance in the air,
They weave the stories of love and care.

Mysteries beckon from the depths of night,
Chasing the dreams that twinkle so bright.
A journey etched in the starlit beams,
Where every moment is stitched with dreams.

With dawn's soft light, the travelers find,
The secrets of phosphors aligned.
Each path reveals what once lay concealed,
In journeys where hearts have gently healed.

So tread the paths of the phosphor glow,
And whisper your wishes to winds that blow.
For journeys loved will forever last,
In luminous tales of the present and past.

A Tapestry of Flickering Dreams

In the quiet hours when twilight sighs,
We craft a tapestry beneath starry skies.
Threads of silver and shades of gold,
Weaving the dreams that each heart holds.

Every flicker a story, each glimmer a song,
A dance of the wishes where we all belong.
Upon the loom of the night so deep,
A fabric of hopes where love will seep.

With gentle fingers, we spin and twist,
The colors of moments that softly persist.
In shadows we stitch what daylight forgot,
Fleeting dreams wrapped in the warmth of thought.

Let the threads guide you through nights so fair,
A whisper of magic in the crisp night air.
For within this tapestry, a world awaits,
Where dreams are alive behind whispering gates.

So gather your dreams, let them take flight,
In the fabric of night, where all is right.
The tapestry blooms with each heartbeat's gleam,
In the vast expanse of flickering dreams.

The Chromatic Thread of Twilight's Dance

In twilight's embrace, colors collide,
From pink to indigo, the horizons glide.
A dance of hues painted on the sky,
As daylight bows and night draws nigh.

The chromatic thread weaves tales untold,
Of adventures embarked and hearts yet bold.
With each shade brushed by the evening's hand,
A symphony of colors both gentle and grand.

Stars outline secrets in shimmering light,
As the world begins to twinkle at night.
From the depths of shadows, dreams take their stand,
With pastel whispers that guide the hand.

Through lavender whispers and cobalt sighs,
The twilight holds magic where the heart lies.
In the tapestry spun by fading sun,
Every moment cherished, each battle won.

So let your spirit dance, let colors flow,
In the twilight's arms, where the magic grows.
For in every hue, a story enchants,
Beneath the canvas of twilight's dance.

The Luminous Echoes of Nightfall

As shadows deepen and day turns gray,
The luminous echoes begin to play.
A song of the stillness, a whisper so low,
In the cradle of night, let your spirit grow.

Stars glisten brightly, like scattered dreams,
Reflecting the wonders of life's gentle themes.
With every flicker, they beckon us near,
A symphony played for those who will hear.

In the hush of the evening, magic unfolds,
With stories of bravery and legends of old.
The echoes of nightfall, a soothing refrain,
A lullaby woven through joy and pain.

So dance to the rhythm of moon's tender light,
Let luminous echoes guide you through night.
For in every glow, a spark of the past,
In the silence of night, our memories last.

Embrace the enchantment, let worries take flight,
In the luminous echoes, find peace in the night.
For within such moments, magic is born,
In the heart of the night, a new world is sworn.

www.ingramcontent.com/pod-product-compliance
Ingram Content Group UK Ltd.
Pitfield, Milton Keynes, MK11 3LW, UK
UKHW021450280125
4335UKWH00035B/474